Collins

Tree of Life 1

A Course on Environmental Studies

Dinu Raheja
Lipika Ghosh

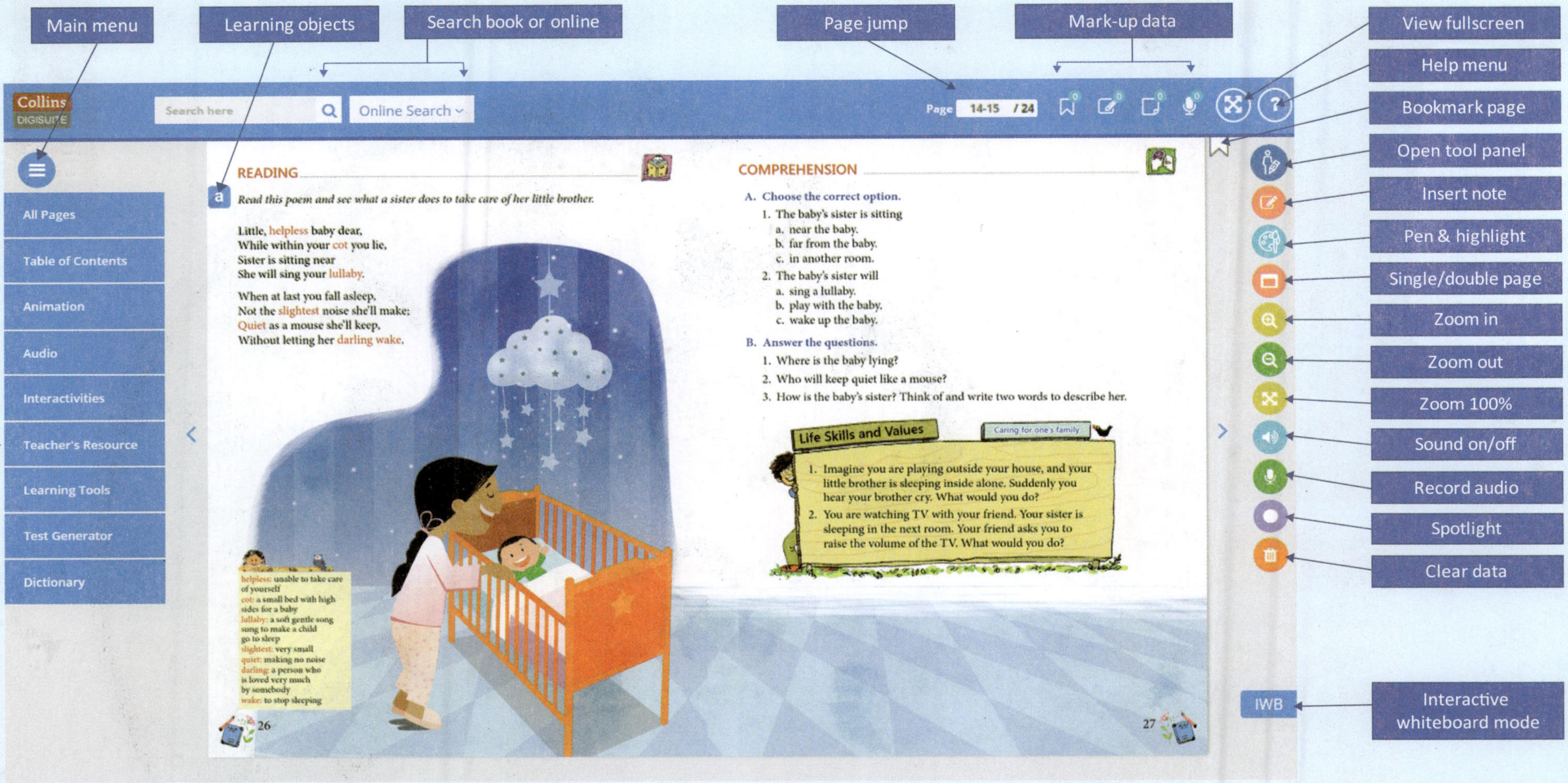

Student + Teacher			Teacher-only	
a animations	**ia** activities	**g** games	**lp** lesson plans	**tn** teacher's notes
ilt instructor-led tutorials	**w** worksheets	**v** videos	**w** worksheets	**ak** answer keys
	audio			

Preface

Tree of Life Updated Edition is an engaging and innovative course on Environmental Studies for classes 1 to 5. It adopts a multidisciplinary approach to ensure holistic learning for young learners. This series of five books adheres to the National Education Policy, 2020. An interactive and learner-centric course, *Tree of Life* has planned pedagogical elements that help learners connect social, cultural and scientific concepts with real-life situations. Promoting experiential learning, learners are encouraged to explore their immediate world and foster environmental awareness. The well-graded content has been created keeping in mind several goals—easy readability, accuracy and creativity. At the same time it empowers learners towards higher levels of academic scholarship.

The concepts in the series are presented simply, supplemented by colourful pictures and illustrations. Varied key features in the series hone learning skills.

- Multidisciplinary and a holistic education—Exploration Station, Cross connect
- Life skills and making ethical decisions—Learn the ropes
- Creativity, art integration, creating joyful classrooms—Put your heads together
- Organic living—Poster, United Nations Sustainability Development Goals
- A rootedness and pride in India—Our Heritage
- Inquiry-based, discovery-based, discussion-based, and analysis-based learning—Get the ball rolling, Clued in, Give it a shot
- Application and problem-solving—Think through, Covid-19 Safety
- Exploratory activities and experiential learning—Why it Works
- Moving towards real understanding and towards learning how to learn—Wrap up
- Assessment—Brush up

It is our endeavour to help the learners develop a responsible attitude towards the preservation of their environment.

- Authors

About the authors

Dinu Raheja, an innovative educationist and administrator, recipient of the International Teacher's Award, has over 15 years of teaching experience in Indian and international schools. Formerly, Middle School Incharge, Sanskriti School, New Delhi, she is currently Program Director with The Global Education & Leadership Foundation (tGELF). Dinu also facilitates teacher leadership development workshops.

Lipika Ghosh has over 25 years of teaching experience at St. Xavier's School Hazaribagh, Sardar Patel Vidyalaya, New Delhi and Sanskriti School, New Delhi. She has used innovative teaching methodology to make science a process of discovery interspersed with anecdotes for learners. Lipika has taught analytical skills and inculcated awareness of social issues amongst learners through science.

Key Features

Tree of Life Updated Edition is an engaging and innovative course on Environmental Studies for classes 1 to 5. The series adheres to the National Education Policy, 2020 and adopts a multidisciplinary approach to enable holistic learning.

Get the ball rolling has compelling pre-teaching warm-up tasks to arouse interest in the topic.

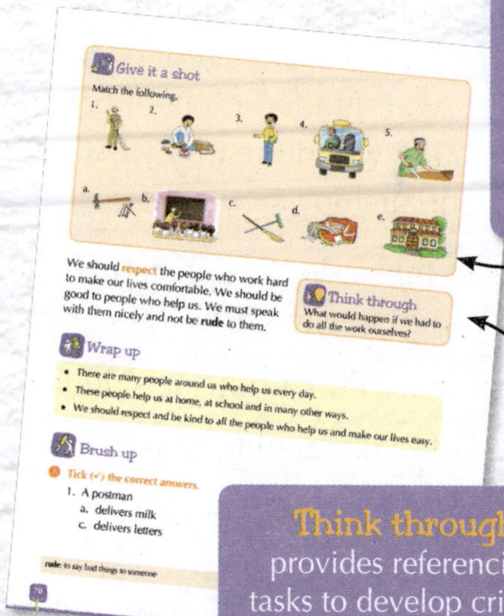

Give it a shot promotes experiential learning through application-based activities.

Think through provides referencing tasks to develop critical thinking skills of the learners.

Clued in provides interesting additional facts for extended learning.

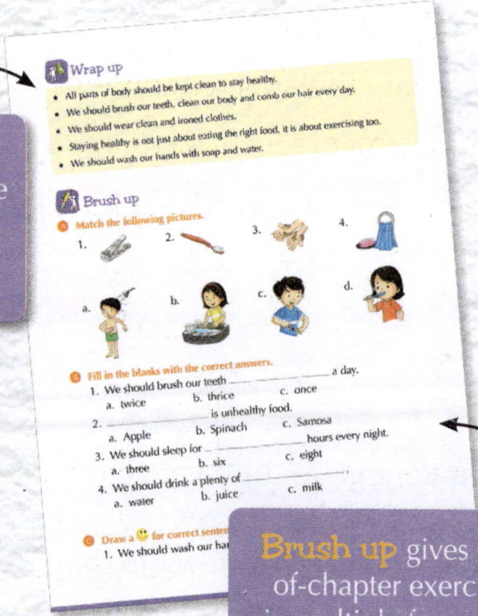

Wrap up provides a ready reckoner to reinforce the concepts taught for comprehensive learning.

Brush up gives end-of-chapter exercises in multiple formats to facilitate assessment.

Learn the ropes provides activities for application of 21st century life skills.

Put your heads together provides group projects to strengthen teamwork and cooperative learning.

Cross connect tasks promote cross-disciplinary and integrated learning.

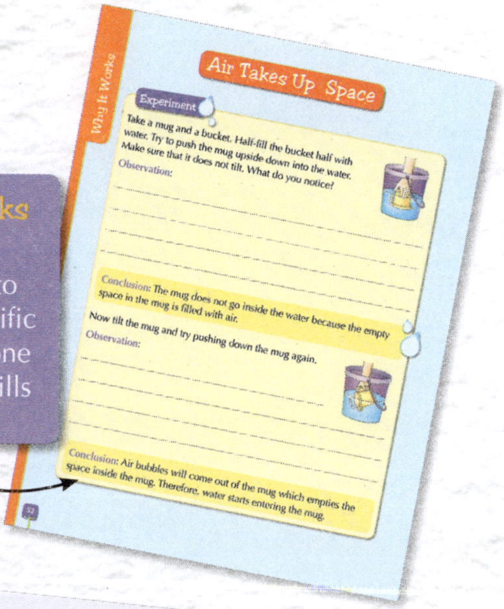

Why It Works provides experiments to promote scientific temper and hone observation skills of learners.

Exploration Station provides case studies for comprehensive knowledge.

Our Heritage provides snippets of information about the heritage of India and encourages learners to preserve it.

Suggested Assessments at the end of the book facilitate cumulative assessment.

Covid-19 Safety teaches students to stay safe and healthy.

United Nations Sustainability Development Goals featured in specific sections to achieve a just and equitable world for all.

Poster on 5Rs sensitizes learners towards their surroundings and creates awareness about sustainability of the environment.

Contents

1 All About Me

Get the ball rolling

Look at the pictures. Talk about them in class.

Hello, I am Aarayna.

I am a girl.

I am six years old.

Hello, I am Aarav.

I am a boy.

I am six years old.

Aarayna and Aarav have said something about themselves.

Now say something about yourself.

My name is ....

I am a .... girl/boy.

Paste your photograph here

I am .... years old.

My birthday is on ....

I study in class ....

Aarayna and Aarav are **friends**. They go to the same school and study in the same class.

Aarayna calls Aarav, Aaru. It is his **nickname**. Do you have a nickname?

Draw a picture of yourself and your friend here.

Think through

What are the differences between you and your best friend?

Have you seen your friends wear cards in school?

These cards are called **identity cards**. They tell us a few things about the person wearing it, such as his or her name, class and birthday.

Now, write about yourself and paste your photograph to complete the identity card.

School logo	Name: ....
	....
Paste photograph here	Class: ....
	Roll Number: ....
	Date of Birth: ....
	School: ....

nickname: pet name of people

Things We Like to Do

We like to do many different things. The things that we enjoy the most are our **favourite** things.

Write your favourite things here:

Colour: ....

Toy: .... Story: ....

Clued in

All of us are different from each other. We look different from each other. Our choices and likes are also different, which makes us special.

Give it a shot

What are these children doing? Tick (✓) the activities you like to do.

1. Playing football

2. Reading

3. Painting

4. Swimming

5. Cycling

6. Skipping

I also like to ....

Wrap up

- Those who study in my class are my friends.
- Identity cards tell us name, age, class and birthday of the person wearing it.
- We like to do different things.
- Things we enjoy the most are our favourite things.

favourite: something liked more than others of the same kind

Brush up

A **Tick (✓) the odd one out in each set.**

1.

 a. ☐

 b. ☐

 c. ☐

 d. ☐

2.

 a. ☐

 b. ☐

 c. ☐

 d. ☐

3.

a. ☐

 b. ☐

 c. ☐

 d. ☐

4.

 a. ☐

 b. ☐

 c. ☐

 d. ☐

B **Write the name of your best friend and his or her five favourite things.**

....

....

C **Answer these questions.**

1. What do you like to eat?
2. What is your weight and height?
3. Write four things that you do not like.

Learn the ropes

Take a sheet of paper and write your full name, your parent's name, your address and telephone numbers of your parents and grandparents. Keep the paper in your school bag.

Put your heads together

Work in pairs. Make a list of food, games, colours and songs that you like and do not like. Compare the list with your partners' to find out how different are you from each other.

Cross connect

Toothbrush painting

Things required: An old toothbrush, kitchen strainer, water paints, stencils of animals, flowers or any other shape, a plain white drawing sheet, old newspaper and tape

1. Cover the work area with a newspaper. Begin by putting a tape at the back of the stencil and press it firmly on the sheet.
2. Hold the kitchen strainer so that it does not touch the paper directly.
3. Dip a toothbrush in one colour and shake off the excess paint. Start brushing across the strainer so that the paint is sprayed around the shapes.
4. Rinse the toothbrush with water while changing colours.
5. Remove the strainer and the stencils and let the drawing sheet dry. Your toothbrush painting is ready.

2 My Body

Get the ball rolling

How do we hear things? Which part of our body do we use to see?

Our body has different parts. Look at the pictures below and learn the names of the different parts of the body.

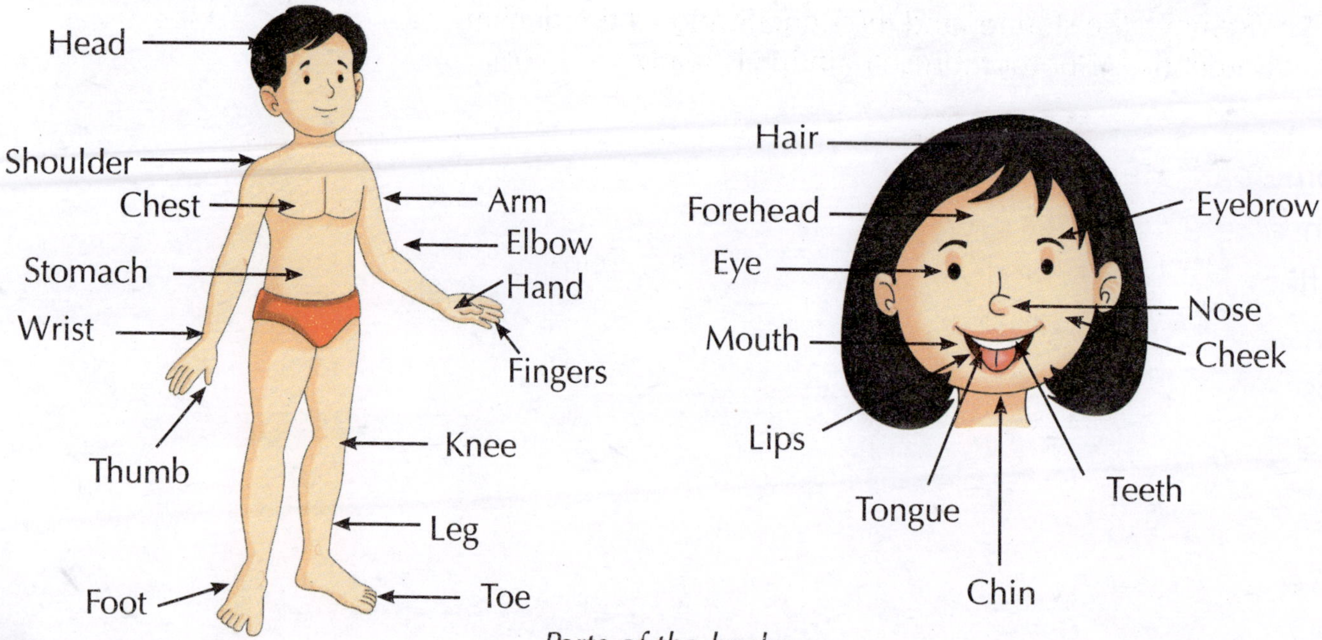

Parts of the body

We use different parts of our body to do different things.

We can **stand**, **walk**, **run** and **jump** with the help of our legs and feet.

Think through

Which part of the body do you use to chew food?

Stand

Walk

Run

Jump

We can do many things with our arms, hands and fingers. Some of them are **eating**, **holding**, **brushing** and **painting**.

Eating

Holding

Brushing

Painting

We use both hands and legs to do activities like **swimming** and **dancing**.

Swimming

Sense Organs

Some parts of our body help us to feel and sense things around us. They are called **sense organs**. We have five sense organs. They are eyes, ears, nose, tongue and skin. They help us to see, hear, smell, taste and feel.

Sense organs

The five sense organs have different functions.

We **see** with our **eyes**.

We **hear** with our **ears**.

We **smell** with our **nose**.

We **taste** with our **tongue**.

We **touch** and **feel** through our **skin**.

Clued in

Our tongue helps us to taste salty, sweet, sour and bitter things.

Give it a shot

Look at these pictures and write down the sense organ that we use to do these activities.

1. ....

2. ....

3. ....

4. ....

5. ....

Wrap up

- Our body has different parts.
- We use different parts of our body to do different things.
- Sense organs are the parts of our body that help us see, feel and sense things around us.
- The five sense organs are eyes, ears, nose, tongue and skin.

Brush up

A Fill in the blanks. Draw and colour these parts of the body.

1. I have .... nose.
2. I have .... fingers.
3. I have .... mouth.
4. I have .... head.
5. I have .... eyes.

B Tick (✓) the correct answers.

1. I smell with my ....
   a. mouth   b. nose   c. eyes
2. I hear with my ....
   a. ears   b. lips   c. neck
3. I write with my ....
   a. mouth   b. ears   c. hands
4. I walk with my ....
   a. tongue   b. legs   c. hands

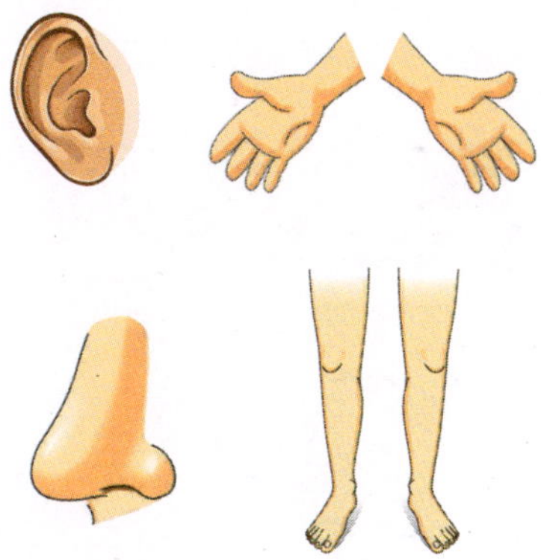

C Answer these questions.

1. What work do we do with our hands?
2. How many sense organs are there in our body? Name them.
3. Name the parts of the body that we use to do the following activities.

a. Eat	....	d. Watch television	....
b. Kick	....	e. Listen to music	....
c. Crawl	....	f. Run	....

Learn the ropes

Observe a bird, a dog, a cat and an ant. Think and write which part of the body these animals use to move. Which of their body parts are in pairs?

Put your heads together

Form two groups in class. One group can draw pictures of different parts of the body and the other group will guess the names and explain the function of the part of body. Take turns and let the other group draw pictures too.

Cross connect

Collect toys, clothes, books and any other item that you do not need or do not use anymore. Bring these things to the school and talk to your teacher about helping you put up a donation stall. You can name your stall and put up your favourite items for display.

3 Healthy and Clean

Get the ball rolling

Why do we need to wash our hands? Talk about this in class.

We know that our body is made up of different parts. All body parts should be kept clean to stay **healthy**.

3 GOOD HEALTH AND WELL-BEING

Keeping Our Body Clean

We should brush our teeth twice a day, once in the morning and once at night before going to bed.

We should take bath every day to keep our body clean. We should also comb our hair.

We should wear clean clothes and give dirty clothes for washing.

We should bathe everyday

We should brush our teeth

healthy: having good health and not likely to become ill

We should clip our nails and keep them short and clean. When we eat with dirty nails, **germs** go inside our body.

We should change our clothes before going to bed. We should always go to bed in clean clothes.

We should clip our nails

We should go to bed in clean clothes

Think through

Why should we change our clothes before going to sleep?

Keeping Our Body Healthy

Staying healthy means doing things that are good for our body. We should follow some good habits to be healthy and strong.

- We should wash our hands with soap and water before and after eating food and every time we use the bathroom.
- We should eat healthy food. Healthy food gives us **energy** and helps us grow. We should also eat food on time.
- We should drink plenty of water every day.
- Staying healthy is not just about eating the right food. It is about exercising too. Exercising keeps our body fit.
- Our body needs rest too. We should go to bed and wake up on time. We should sleep for eight hours every night.

We should wash our hands before and after eating

Clued in

Burgers, french fries, samosas and chips are unhealthy food. They are also known as **junk food**. We should avoid eating them.

Give it a shot

Take a sheet of paper and paste pictures of food that you love to eat. You can also draw and colour them. Take your teacher's help and draw a ☺ for healthy food and a ☹ for unhealthy or junk food.

germs: very small living things which can make us sick; **energy**: the ability to do work

Wrap up

- All parts of our body should be kept clean to stay healthy.
- We should brush our teeth, clean our body and comb our hair every day.
- We should wear clean and ironed clothes.
- Staying healthy is not just about eating the right food, it is about exercising too.
- We should wash our hands with soap and water.

Brush up

A Match the following.

1. 

2. 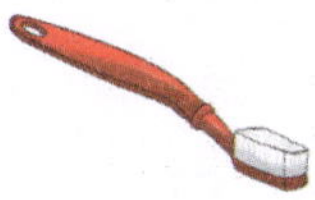

3. 

4. 

a. 

b. 

c. 

d. 

B Fill in the blanks with the correct answers.

1. We should brush our teeth .... a day.
   a. twice b. thrice c. once
2. .... is unhealthy food.
   a. Apple b. Spinach c. Samosa
3. We should sleep for .... hours every night.
   a. three b. six c. eight
4. We should drink plenty of ....
   a. water b. juice c. milk

C Draw a ☺ for correct sentences and a ☹ for the incorrect ones.

1. We should wash our hands only after eating.

2. We should take bath every day to keep our body clean.
3. We should not clip our nails.
4. Exercising keeps our body fit.

D Answer these questions.

1. Why should we bathe every day?
2. Why is washing hands important?
3. Why should we clip our nails?
4. Write four ways to stay healthy and strong.

Learn the ropes

Talk about the importance of exercise for a healthy body in class. You can do a few exercises while trying to make your point. Make a simple routine of these exercises and try to do them every day.

Put your heads together

Follow the leader

Form groups and select a team leader for each group. The leader would perform physical activities such as jumping, dancing, hopping, clapping and skipping. The other group has to perform these activities in the same sequence as the leader does. The group that does the activity in correct sequence scores a point. Take turns and give all the group members a chance to be the team leader.

Cross connect

Pour a drop of sanitizer and glitter on your hands. Rub your hands until there is glitter all over. Walk around the classroom and shake hands with your classmates. Touch a few objects. Now look at your hands and look around. What do you see? There is glitter all over your hands, the hands of the people you shook hands with and even on the objects you touched. Germs spread like the glitter on hands, except they cannot be seen and are bad for our health.

4 My Family

Get the ball rolling

Who are the people that stay with you in your house? Are there many people in your house?

A small family

Mother, father and children living together are a **family**. Our mother and father are our **parents** and our brothers and sisters are our **siblings**. Some families are small and some are large.

Small Families

Families in which parents live with their one or more than one children are **small families**. They are also called **nuclear families**.

Clued in

Some families are very small. They only have one parent and children. The parent can be a father or a mother. Such a family is called a single-parent family.

Large Families

Families in which grandparents, parents, children, uncles, aunts and their children live together in the same house are called **large families**. They are also called **joint families**.

A large family

Family Relations

Our mother's father and our father's father are our **grandfathers**. Our mother's mother and our father's mother are our **grandmothers**. The brothers of our father and our mother are our **uncles**. The sisters of our father and our mother are our **aunts**. The children of our uncles and aunts are our **cousins**. **Grandparents**, uncles, aunts and our cousins are our **relatives**.

Family relations can be shown on a family tree. Let us look at Tanya's family tree to understand this.

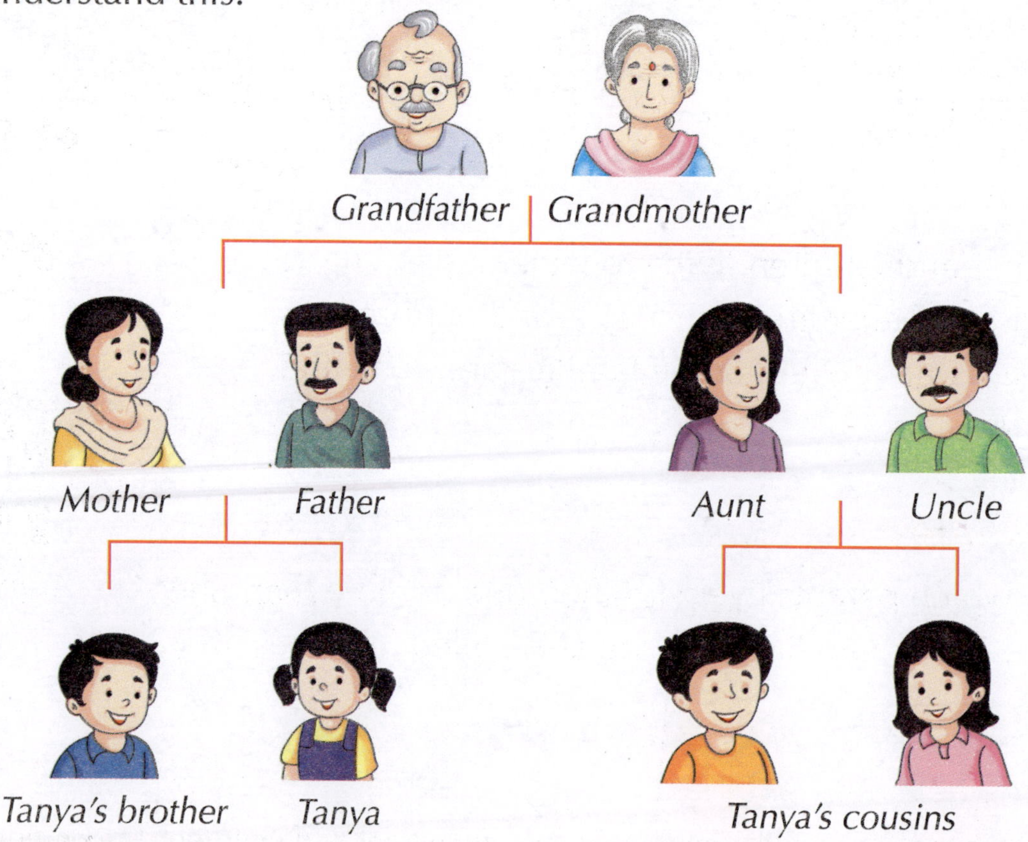

grandparents: parents of our parents

Write the names of your family members and paste their photographs to complete your family tree.

Family tree

Family is Important

Family is very important. We get love and care from our family. Our parents look after us when we fall ill. They help us, keep us safe and healthy and give us things that we need. We learn good manners from our family. We should help our family members. We should love and respect them.

Think through

Your family does so much for you. How do you help your family?

Give it a shot

Look at the picture and write the correct letter in the boxes.

1. This is my brother. ☐
2. This is my grandfather. ☐
3. This is my mother. ☐
4. This is my grandmother. ☐
5. This is my father. ☐
6. This is my sister. ☐
7. This is my pet. ☐

Wrap up

- We live with our parents, brother and sister as a family.
- A family can be small or large.
- In a small family, the parents and the children live together.
- In a large family, grandparents, parents, children, uncles, aunts and cousins live together in the same house.
- Our family gives us love and care and keeps us safe.
- We should respect and love our family.

Brush up

A Draw a ☺ for correct sentences and a ☹ for the incorrect ones.

1. A nuclear family is a large family. ◯
2. Uncles, aunts and cousins live together in a joint family. ◯
3. Our father and mother are our siblings. ◯
4. The parents of our parents are our grandparents. ◯
5. We get love and care from our family. ◯

B Match the images with their descriptions.

1. 	a. Nuclear family
2. 	b. Grandmother
3. 	c. Joint family
4. 	d. Single parent family
5. 	e. Grandfather

C Answer these questions.

1. Name the members of your family who live in the same house with you.
2. What is a nuclear family?

3. What is a joint family?
4. Write two things that you do as a family together.
5. Who are our cousins?

Learn the ropes

Our family loves us. We should give our family members love and care too. One way of doing this is by saying thank you to our parents and grandparents. Write two more ways in which you can show that you love and care for your family.

Put your heads together

Form two groups. Bring the photographs of your parents to the class. Ask your group members to do the same. Make a group photo album and write your name and the parent's name below each set. Keep the album in your class.

Cross connect

Birthday Card

Make a birthday card for any of your family members.

Material required: thick coloured paper, sketch pens, glue

* Take a sheet of thick paper and fold it into half.
* With the help of an adult, select a photograph of the family member and paste it on the card.
* You can even draw a picture.
* Draw balloons or flowers to decorate around the picture.
* Write your birthday message inside.

5 Plants Around Us

Get the ball rolling

Look at the plants in this picture. Talk about them in class.

Plants are of different types. Some plants are big and some are small. We depend on plants for many things.

Types of Plants

Tall and big plants are called **trees**. They have thick and strong stems. Mango tree, banyan, neem, peepal and coconut tree are some trees.

Mango tree

Banyan

Neem

Peepal

Coconut tree

There are some plants that are much smaller than trees. Their stems are hard and woody. They are called **shrubs**. They are also known as **bushes**. Rose, hibiscus and tulsi are shrubs.

Rose

Hibiscus

Tulsi

Clued in

Tea plant is a shrub. Its leaves are dried and used to make tea.

Some plants are very small. They have weak, soft and green stems. They are called **herbs**. Spinach, mint, coriander and parsley are herbs.

Mint

Spinach

Coriander

Some plants have very weak stems and they need support for their stems to grow. These plants are called **climbers**. Some common climbers are grapevine, pea plant and money plant.

Grapevine

Money plant

There are some weak plants which grow along the ground. These plants are called **creepers**. Pumpkin and watermelon are common creepers.

Pumpkin

Watermelon

Air, **water** and **sunlight** are very important for plants. They help the plants to make their own food.

Think through

Why are seeds important for a plant?

Give it a shot

Look around and make a list of five big and five small plants in your notebook. Write their names and find out whether they are trees, shrubs or herbs. Draw or paste their pictures.

Uses of Plants

Plants are useful to us in many ways.

- Plants clean the air to help us breathe.
- We get food from plants. They give us **fruits** and **vegetables**.
- We get **food grains** like rice and wheat from plants. We also get **pulses** like dal and gram from them.
- Some plants produce **nuts**. We eat almonds and cashew nuts which are seeds of plants.

- Plants give us **tea**, **coffee** and **sugar**.
- Some plants give us **spices** like cloves and cardamom.

- We get **oils** used for cooking from seeds of plants.

- Plants like tulsi and neem are used for making **medicines**.

- We get **cotton** and **jute** from plants. Cotton is used to make clothes and quilts. Jute is used for making mats and bags.

- Rubber from rubber trees is used to make footballs, erasers and tyres.
- Plants give us flowers which are used to make perfumes.

- We get paper from plants.
- We get wood from trees. Wood is used to make furniture.

Wrap up

- Plants are of different types.
- Tall, big plants with thick and strong stems are called trees.
- Shrubs and herbs are small plants.
- Weak plants that climb up a support to grow are called climbers.
- Weak plants that grow along the ground are called creepers.
- Plants are useful to us in many ways.

Brush up

A **Match the types of plants with their examples.**

1.	Creeper	a.	
2.	Tree	b.	
3.	Herb	c.	
4.	Shrub	d.	
5.	Climber	e.	

B **Draw a 🙂 for the correct sentences and a ☹ for incorrect ones.**

1. Weak plants which grow along the ground are known as creepers.
2. Plants which have weak green stems are called shrubs.
3. Shrubs are also known as bushes.
4. Flowers are used to make tea.

C **Answer these questions.**

1. How many types of plants are there? Name them.
2. What is the difference between climbers and creepers?
3. Mention any five uses of plants.

Learn the ropes

Find out the names of plants that grow at your home or school. Write three ways in which you can take care of them.

Put your heads together

Collect any pieces of extra coloured paper or chart paper from your home or school. In groups, make bookmarks using them. With the help of your teacher cut them out neatly in the shape of a bookmark. Colour them. Share your bookmarks with your classmates.

Cross connect

Wrapping Sheet

Things required: a thin chart paper, ladies' fingers, colours

Take a thin chart paper. Now take one lady finger and some paint. Cut one end of the lady finger. Dip it in paint and make prints on the chart paper. Use the paper to wrap gifts.

6 Animals Around Us

Get the ball rolling

Have you ever wondered about life under the sea? Talk about it in class.

There are many kinds of animals around us. Some animals are big and some are small. Birds, fish and insects are animals too.

Big Animals and Small Animals

Animals like elephants, giraffes, whales, ostriches and bears are **big animals**.

Giraffe

Ostrich

Whale

Elephant

Animals such as dogs, cats, porcupines, squirrels and rabbits are **small animals**.

Porcupine

Rabbit

Squirrel

Dog

Cat

Birds and Insects

Birds are animals with wings, feathers and two legs. They have beaks and no teeth. Most birds can fly. Parrots, owls, pigeons and eagles are some birds that can fly. Pigeons and sparrows eat grains. They also eat insects. Eagles and owls feed on small animals.

Parrot

Owl

Eagle

> **Clued in**
>
> Birds like ostrich, kiwi and penguins cannot fly.

Insects are very small animals. Most of them have six or more legs and wings to fly. Mosquitoes, butterflies, houseflies and grasshoppers are some insects. Some insects like silverfish and louse do not have wings.

Mosquito

Butterfly

Grasshopper

Places Animals Live in

Different types of animals live in different places.

Some animals live on land and are called **land animals**. Animals like lions, camels, zebras, horses and deer live on land.

> **Think through**
>
> In zoos, animals are kept in cages. Do you think they are happy there?

Lion

Camel

Horse

Zebra

Some animals live in water. They are called **water animals**. They cannot live without water. Fish, jellyfish, octopus and dolphins are water animals. The whale is the largest water animal.

Crab

Fish

Starfish

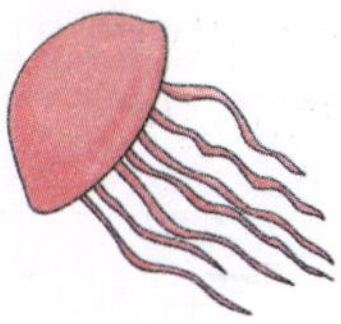

Jellyfish

Turtle

Frogs, crocodiles, turtles and ducks are some animals that live in water as well as on land.

Frog

Crocodile

Some animals live with us in our homes. They are like our friends.

We call them **pets**. Dogs, cats, fish and parrots are pets. We love and take care of our pets.

Like human beings and plants, it is also important to **protect** and take care of animals.

Give it a shot

Write the names of two of each:

1. Animals living on land ....
2. Animals living in water ....
3. Animals living both on land and in water ....

Paste their pictures in your notebook.

Wrap up

- Animals are of different sizes, some are big and some are small.
- Elephants and giraffes are big animals and squirrel and rabbit are small animals.
- Birds are animals with wings, feathers and two legs.
- Insects are very small animals. Most of them have six or more legs.
- Some animals live on land, some in water and some live both on land and in water.
- Lions and horses live on land, fish and dolphins live in water and crocodiles and frogs lives both on land and in water.
- Some animals live with us in our homes, they are called our pets. We must protect and take care of animals.

protect: keep safe from harm or injury

Brush up

A Match the following.

1.	Land animal	a.	
2.	Bird	b.	
3.	Water animal	c.	
4.	Land and water animal	d.	
5.	Insect	e.	

B Fill in the blanks with correct answers.

1. Animals that live in .... are called water animals.
   a. forests   b. water   c. homes
2. The whale is the largest .... animal.
   a. land   b. tree   c. water
3. Insects have .... legs.
   a. two   b. less than four   c. six or more
4. .... are animals with feathers.
   a. Insects   b. Water animals   c. Birds

C Answer these questions.

1. What are water animals? Give two examples.
2. What are insects? Give two examples.
3. What are land animals? Give two examples.
4. What are birds? Give two examples.

Learn the ropes

Visit a local zoo or a farm. Write four lines about the animal you liked the most. Talk about how it looks, the sound it makes and the type of food it eats. Draw or paste pictures of the animal in your notebook.

Put your heads together

Let us write an animal poem

Work in groups. Choose an animal, bird or an insect and write a short poem about it. You can form sentences using the following clues:

Line 1: Name of the animal

Line 2: Two words to describe the animal

Line 3: Where does it live? Form a complete one sentence

Line 4: Two words to describe what kind of animal it is

Line 5: Sound it makes

You can ask your teacher for help or for more clues.

Cross connect

Form two groups. The first group will mimic the sound of an animal. The second group will guess the name of the animal. The group with the most number of correct guesses wins.

7 Food We Eat

Get the ball rolling

Do you have likes and dislikes about food? Discuss them in class.

All of us need food as it helps us to live and grow. After we play, study or work, we feel hungry, weak and tired. Food gives us **energy** to work as well as to play.

Meals

We eat three **meals** a day. Food we eat in the morning after we wake up is called **breakfast**. We should have a glass of milk every day in the morning before or with breakfast.

Milk is good for our health. It makes our bones and teeth strong.

Food we eat in the afternoon is called **lunch**. We should eat rice, chapatti, dal, vegetables, curd and chicken or fish.

energy: power to do things; **meal**: the food we eat at certain times of the day

Food we eat at night before going to bed is called **dinner**. Dinner should always be light.

Breakfast

Lunch

Dinner

All meals should be eaten at the right time. It makes our body strong and healthy. Members of a family should eat together at least one meal in a day.

Clued in

Eating too many chocolates and sweets is not good for health.

Give it a shot

Write what did you eat for these meals yesterday.

Breakfast: .... , ...

Lunch: .... , ...

Dinner: .... , ...

Did you eat anything in between?

Take your teachers' or parents' help to check whether you are eating healthy food or not.

Food from Plants and Animals

We get food from plants and animals. The right kind of food makes us healthy and strong.

Think through

Why should we not eat food that is not covered?

We get fruits such as orange, mango, apple, pineapple and strawberry from plants.

Orange

Pineapple

Strawberries

Mango

We get vegetables such as tomato, brinjal and cucumber from plants.

Tomato

Brinjal

Cucumber

Pumpkin

Corn

Beetroot

We get **cereals** or **food grains** from plants such as rice and wheat.

Rice

Wheat

Seeds of some plants are called **pulses**. Bengal gram, green gram and kidney beans are some examples of pulses.

Bengal gram

Green gram

Kidney beans

We get food from animals too. We get milk from animals. We make more things from milk such as butter, cheese, yogurt and ice cream. These are called **milk products**. We get honey from the honey bees. We get eggs, chicken and meat from animals.

Honey

Cheese

Yoghurt

Milk

Eggs

cereals: wheat, rice, corn, etc.

Good Food Habits

We should eat fresh food. Food eaten in the right amount is **healthy food**.

We should chew our food well and slowly.

We should not overeat.

We should eat slowly.

We must eat food that is covered.

We must always wash our hands before and after eating.

We should drink six to eight glasses of water every day.

We should never waste or throw food.

Wrap up

- All of us need food as it helps us to grow.
- We usually eat three meals a day. They are breakfast, lunch and dinner.
- Our food comes from plants as well as from animals.
- We should always eat fresh food.
- We should drink six to eight glasses of water daily.

Brush up

A Match the pictures of food to their source.

1. 
Honey

2. 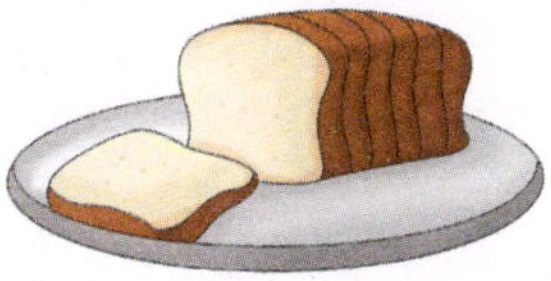
Bread

3. 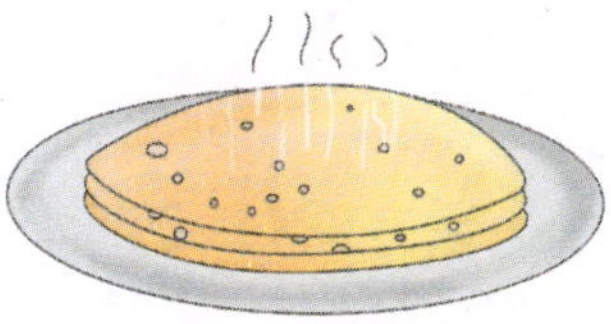
Chapatti

4. 
Cheese

5. 
Butter

Plants

Animals

9. 
Apple

6. 
Fruits and vegetables

7. 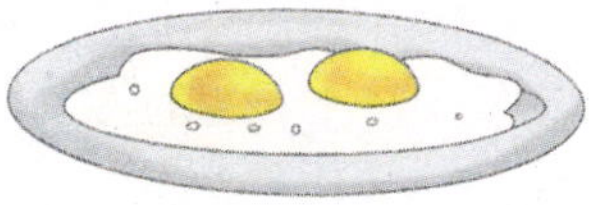
Eggs

8. 
Rice

B Fill in the blanks with the correct answers.

1. .... helps us to live and grow.
   a. Water b. Food c. Toys
2. Eating the right kind of food makes us healthy and ....
   a. strong b. weak c. fat
3. We should always wash our hands before and after ....
   a. playing b. singing c. eating

4. Milk makes our .... and teeth strong.
   a. hair   b. muscles   c. bones

C Answer these questions.

1. Why is food important for us?
2. What are the different meals we eat?
3. Write three good food habits.

Learn the ropes

We should always take food in small helpings so that we can finish it and not waste food. What are the other ways in which you can try to save food?

Put your heads together

Work in pairs. Make two cut-outs—one of a tree and the other of an animal. Draw pictures of food we get from animals on the correct cut-outs. Share the cut-outs with your classmates.

Cross connect

Tommy is lost in the maze.
Help Timmy find Tommy so that they can have lunch with their mother.

8 Our Clothes

Get the ball rolling

Look at these pictures. Talk about them in the class.

We wear clothes to protect ourselves from heat, cold and rain. They also keep us safe from insect bites, dust and dirt. We wear different kinds of clothes in different seasons.

Clothes We Wear

When it is hot, we wear clothes that keep us cool. **Cotton clothes** keep our body cool. Some clothes we wear in the summer are skirts, shorts, t-shirts and dresses.

We wear cotton clothes in summer

When it is cold, we wear **woollen clothes** that keep us warm. These clothes are thick and are made of wool. We get wool from sheep.

We wear woollen clothes in winter

We wear raincoats when it rains

We wear clothes that keep us dry when it is **rainy**. We wear raincoats and carry umbrellas during this time. We also wear **gumboots** when it rains a lot. They keep our feet dry when it rains.

> **Think through**
> How do umbrellas and raincoats keep us dry?

We must always wear clean clothes. Wearing clean clothes keep us healthy. We do not always need new clothes. We should reuse our clothes till they no longer fit us.

Uniforms

Sometimes people have to wear special clothes. These are called **uniforms**. People wear different uniforms to work. We also wear uniforms when we go to school.

> **Clued in**
> Kimono is the national dress of Japan. Saree is one of the most popular dresses of India.

Can you make out what work people do by looking at their uniforms? Name these people who help us.

1. .... 2. .... 3. .... 4. ....

Give it a shot

Anya has three separate sections in her cupboard. These are summer section, winter section and rainy day section. Anya's clothes are mixed up in her room. Help Anya clean her room and put her clothes away in the correct section in her cupboard.

Summer	Winter	Rainy day
....	....	....
....	....	....
....	....	....
....	....	....

Wrap up

- We wear clothes to protect ourselves from heat, cold and rain.
- We wear different types of clothes in different seasons.
- We wear cotton clothes in the summer as they keep us cool.
- We wear woollen clothes in the winter as they keep us warm.

Brush up

A Fill in the blanks using the words given in the box.

umbrella	cool	protect	woollen	clean

1. Clothes .... us from the heat and cold.
2. Cotton clothes keep us ....
3. We wear .... clothes in the winter.
4. We should always wear .... clothes.
5. .... keeps us dry in the rainy season.

B Draw a ☺ for true sentences and ☹ for the false ones.

1. We wear sweaters in the rainy season so that we stay dry. ◯
2. We wear special clothes called uniforms to work. ◯
3. We wear cotton clothes in summer. ◯
4. Clothes protect us from heat and rain. ◯
5. A raincoat protects us from rain. ◯

C Answer these questions.

1. What is a uniform?
2. Why do we wear cotton clothes in the summer?
3. What kind of clothes do we wear in the winter? Why?

4. What do we wear in the rainy season?
5. Why should we wear clean clothes?

Learn the ropes

Sometimes our clothes get torn. We can ask a tailor to stitch them again for us. What will you do with clothes that no longer fit you?

Put your heads together

Work in pairs. What kind of clothes do you like to wear? Paste pictures of your favourite clothes on a chart paper. Find out what kind of clothes your parents and siblings like to wear. Paste these pictures on the same chart paper. Talk about them in class.

Cross connect

Do you get ready for school yourself or do your parents help you? Can you button your shirt, skirt or shorts by yourself? Here is an easy way to do it.

- Hold the button with your thumb, first finger and middle finger and then push it through the button slot and straighten it.
- Start with the lower buttons. These are easier to do as you can see the button and the button hole.
- Now work your way up one button at a time, till all the buttons are fastened.

9 Air and Water

Get the ball rolling

Do you know why we need both air and water? Talk about them in class.

Air and water are very important for all living things. We need air as well as water to live. Let us learn more about air, water and their uses.

Air

We cannot see air, but it is present everywhere. Air helps us breathe. We cannot touch or smell air, but we can feel it.

We can feel air

We can feel the air when a fan or a cooler is switched on. We can feel air when we roll down the window in the car and while running in the playground.

Air moves from one place to another. Moving air is called **wind**. When wind moves softly, it is called a **breeze**. Strong wind is called **storm**.

Breeze

Wind

Storm

Need for air

Air helps to move many things. It moves clouds from one place to another.

Air dries clothes.

Air makes the kites fly.

Think through

How can you tell the direction of the wind?

Air makes sailboats move on water.

Air helps birds fly.

Air makes hot balloons rise.

Many things need to be filled with air before they can be used. Objects like balloons, footballs, air pillows, swimming rings and tyres can only be used after they are filled with air.

Give it a shot

Let us do some deep breathing exercises. Ask an elder to help you.

Steps

- Sit in a cross-legged position.
- Press your ears hard using your fingers and close your eyes.
- Breathe in through your nose. Keep your mouth closed.
- Now, breathe out through your nose and start humming like a bumble bee.
- Repeat this twice.

Air Takes Up Space

Experiment

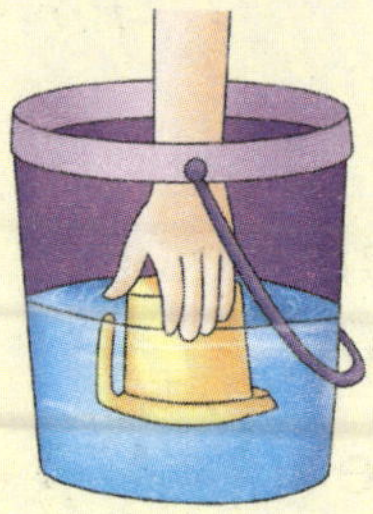

Take a mug and a bucket. Fill half bucket with water. Try to push the mug upside down into the water. Make sure that it does not tilt. What do you notice?

Observation:

Conclusion: The mug does not go inside the water because the empty space in the mug is filled with air.

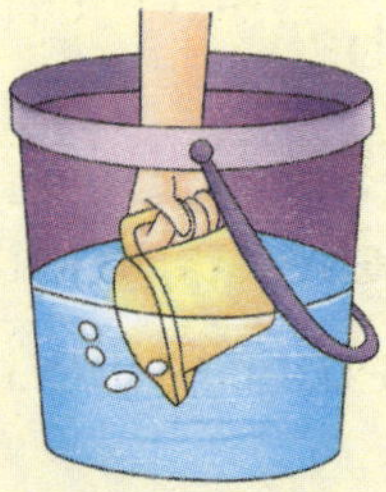

Now tilt the mug and try pushing down the mug again.

Observation:

Conclusion: Air bubbles will come out of the mug which empties the space inside the mug. Therefore, water starts entering the mug.

Water

We need water to live. Just like us, plants and animals also need water to live. Water does not have any colour, taste or smell.

> **Clued in**
>
> Water when cooled in freezer turns into ice. When water is boiled, it turns into steam.

Sources of Water

Rain is the main **source** of water. **Rainwater** fills up the rivers, lakes, ponds, seas and oceans. The water in all these **waterbodies** come either from rain or from the snow on mountains. The snow on mountains melts into water when it gets the warmth of the Sun.

River

Lake

Sea

Water is found **underground** also. We get water from wells, tube wells and hand pumps. We get water at home from all these sources, which reaches us through pipes and taps.

Hand pump

Well

Cooking

Drinking

Uses of water

We use water to do many things. Some of these are drinking, cooking, cleaning, bathing and washing.

source: the place or thing that something comes from or starts at; **waterbodies**: body of water; **underground**: under the surface of the ground

We also need water for putting out fires. We use water for activities like swimming and ice-skating. Plants need water to grow.

Putting out fire

Boat floats on water

Animals need water

Animals and birds also need water to drink and to keep their bodies cool.

6 CLEAN WATER AND SANITATION

Keeping Air and Water Clean

Both air and water should be kept clean.

- **Smoke** coming out from vehicles makes the air dirty. Walking, riding bicycles and using **carpools** help in keeping the air clean.
- Plants clean the air. We should plant trees all around us and take care of them.
- Waste should not be thrown in waterbodies.
- Water can be saved by closing taps when not in use.

Wrap up

* We cannot see air but it is present everywhere. We cannot touch or smell air, but we can feel it.
* We need air to breathe. Plants and animals also need air to breathe.
* Clean water has no colour, no taste and no smell.
* Rain, springs, rivers, lakes, ponds, oceans and seas are some sources of water.
* We need water for many things.
* Both air and water should be kept clean.

smoke: the gas given off by any burning material; **carpool**: if a group of people carpool, they travel to work together in one car and divide the cost between them

Brush up

A Unscramble the words using the clues.

1. NIWD (Moving air) .... D
2. ERRVI (A source of water which flows) .... V ....
3. NIRA (The main source of water) .... I ....
4. ASE (Water in this is salty) .... A
5. ZEBERE (Soft moving wind) B ....
6. TROSM (Strong wind) S ....

B Draw a 🙂 for a correct sentences and ☹ for the incorrect ones.

1. We get water from rain. ○
2. We can smell and touch air. ○
3. Water reaches our homes through pipes and taps. ○
4. Moving air is known as breeze. ○
5. Water is only used for drinking and bathing. ○
6. Air dries the clothes. ○

C Answer these questions.

1. What is wind?
2. Write any four uses of water.
3. How can we keep the air clean?
4. Write the names of four sources of water.

Learn the ropes

Water stored for a long time should not be thrown away. It can be used for watering plants, washing clothes and cleaning floors. Do you or your family members do any of these at home?

Put your heads together

Form four groups. Two groups for air and two for water. Collect pictures about how to keep air and water clean and discuss in class. You can also paste photos of different ways of keeping air and water clean and create charts for display in class.

Cross connect

Make a wind chime

You will need five long sticks or tubes, five strings of equal length and one thick bangle.

1. Take the sticks and tie them to the strings.
2. Then tie the other end of the strings to the bangle.
3. Now, tie a long string at the centre of the bangle for hanging.
4. Your wind chime is ready!

10 Our School

Get the ball rolling

What do you like most about your school? Discuss it in class.

We go to school to learn new things, to make friends and to play. We learn to read and write in school. We also learn singing, dancing and using computers. Our teachers teach us many new things. They also teach us **good manners**.

Principal

The **Principal** is the head of the school and looks after it. The Principal mostly works in his or her office. He or she makes sure that the students learn and enjoy in the school.

Places in a School

There are many different places in a school.

good manners: to behave well with other people

We study in the **classroom**. A school has many classrooms.

Classroom

The teachers keep our notebooks in the **staffroom**. They sit, read and check our notebooks in a staffroom.

Staffroom

We go to the **library** to read books. There are different types of books in the library. The **library teacher** sometimes reads us a story too.

Library

We go to the **computer lab** to learn how to use a computer. We have lots of fun learning to draw and paint on the computer.

Computer lab

Clued in

Phumachangtan Primary School in Tibet is the highest school in the world.

Think through

How do you show respect for your teacher?

The **playground** is where we have the most fun. We play with our friends in the playground. The sports teacher sometimes makes us do **exercises** in the playground.

Playground

exercise: to remain healthy

A school also has **bathrooms** and **drinking water coolers**.

We wear our **uniform** to school. We must be friendly to our classmates and learn to share with them.

We should not dirty our school. We should **respect** and be **polite** to our teachers and all those who help us in the school.

We learn to share with our classmates.

Give it a shot

Tick (✓) the things you learn in a school.

1.  ☐
2.  ☐
3.  ☐
4.  ☐
5.  ☐
6.  ☐
7. 

☐
8.  ☐

Wrap up

- We learn many new things in school.
- A school has many different places like classrooms, staffroom, library, computer lab and a playground.
- We should not dirty our school.

respect: to think good about someone; **polite**: having good manners

* We should respect our teachers and all those who help us.
* We wear uniform to school.

Brush up

A **Fill in the blanks using the words given in the box.**

library	classroom	learn	staffroom	Principal

1. We go to school to .... new things and make new friends.
2. Teachers make us study in a ....
3. Teachers check notebooks in the ....
4. A .... has different types of books.
5. The .... looks after everything in a school.

B **Write the names of the rooms/places where students do these activities.**

1. Learn to use a computer ....
2. Read stories ....
3. Learn to read and write ....
4. Have fun with my friends ....
5. See the Principal working ....

C **Answer these questions.**

1. Why do we go to school?
2. What can we do in a library?
3. Which games do you play with your friends in the playground?
4. What do teachers do in the staffroom?
5. What work does the Principal do?

Learn the ropes

One way to show that we love our school is by keeping our classroom clean and tidy. We must not write on the walls of our classroom or on the desks. We must not throw things on the floor. All the rubbish must be thrown in the dustbin in the classroom. Can you think of two more ways in which you can keep your school and classroom clean?

Put your heads together

You have learnt about the places in a school. Go for a walk around your school with your teacher and try to find the places you read about. Make a list of all things that you see on the way. Talk about it with your teacher once you are back in class.

Cross connect

Start writing your diary. Every day write down three things that you have learnt in school that day. Share and discuss what you have written in the class.

11 Places Around Us

Get the ball rolling

Where do you live? Do you know your home address? Can you name the places near your house?

The houses and the places around our house form our **neighbourhood**. The people who live near our house are our **neighbours**. We see a lot of places such as a park, a school, a hospital, a post office and a market in our neighbourhood. These places make it easy to live in a neighbourhood.

A neighbourhood

Market

A **market** is a place from where we can buy everyday things. Having a market in the neighbourhood is important because we do not need to go very far to buy things we need. A market has many **shops** that sell different things.

Think through

Name three things you can buy from the market in your neighbourhood.

There are many other places in a neighbourhood.

We play in the **park**.

We send letters from the **post office**. We can also buy **stamps** and envelopes from a post office.

We go to the **hospital** when we are sick or badly hurt. The doctor gives us medicines to make us well.

Police officers work in a **police station**. They keep us safe from **criminals**.

We study in the **school**. We learn many new things in school.

We go to the **bus stop** to catch a bus to school or to any other place.

Clued in

Neighbourhoods have different places of worship where people go to pray.

stamp: a small piece of paper with a design on it that you buy and stick on an envelope before you post it;
criminals: people who do actions that harm others

Give it a shot

Match the places in the neighbourhood to the activities that are done there.

1. 

a. I go there to visit a doctor.

2. 

b. I can buy vegetables from this place.

3. 

c. I can take help from police officers in this place.

4. 

d. I can buy stamps from this place.

We should keep our neighbourhood clean and not make it dirty by throwing things on the road outside our house.

We should keep our neighbourhood clean

Wrap up

- The houses and places around our house together form our neighbourhood.
- Market, school, park, hospital, post office, police station and bus stop are some places found in a neighbourhood.
- We should keep our neighbourhood clean.

Brush up

A **Tick (✓) the correct answers.**

1. We go to the (school/bus stop) to study.
2. We can buy fruits and vegetables from the (park/market).
3. We go to the (police station/post office) to send letters and buy stamps.
4. We play with our friends in the (park/police station).
5. We take the school bus from the (hospital/bus stop).

B **Fill in the blanks.**

1. The houses and the area around our house is our ....
2. When we are sick or badly hurt we should go to the ....
3. Police officers work in a ....
4. There are many shops in the .... where we can buy different things.
5. We can send letters from a ....

C **Answer these questions.**

1. Write the names of places in your neighbourhood that:
   a. You visit every day   b. You visit sometimes
2. Why is the market an important place in the neighbourhood?
3. What do the police officers do?
4. Why do we need a hospital?
5. What do we do in a park?

Learn the ropes

Go to the market in your neighbourhood with your parents.

* Make a list of all the shops that you see.
* Note down the names of some of the things that these shops sell.
* Write how many people work in each shop. Talk about your trip around the market in class.

Put your heads together

Work in groups and make your neighbourhood chart. Draw the picture of your house in the middle of the chart. Around the house, paste pictures or draw the places that you have in your neighbourhood. Write two things that you like about your neighbourhood below the pictures.

Cross connect

Do you have a park in your neighbourhood? Do you play in that park? Go to the park in your neighbourhood with your parents. Count the number of swings, slides and benches in the park. Write it down in your notebook and note down the colour of the swings, slides and benches.

12 People Who Help Us

Get the ball rolling

When you reach school, you find your classroom neat and clean. Who do you think cleans them?

There are many people around us who help us. They help us at home, at school and in many other ways.

People Who Help Us at Home

A **paperboy** delivers newspapers to our homes every morning.

A **milkman** delivers milk to our homes every morning.

A **cook** makes food for us.

A **maid** sweeps and cleans our homes and cleans the dishes.

A **car cleaner** cleans our cars with water and soap.

People Who Help Us at School

A **school bus driver** takes us to school every morning and drops us back home after school.

A **school guard** guards our school.

A **teacher** teaches us new things every day.

A **cleaner** sweeps and cleans our school every day. A cleaner uses a **broom** and a **mop** to clean.

A **gardener** looks after the plants in our school so that our school looks green.

Clued in

Film and television actors and singers are people who work to **entertain** us.

entertain: give enjoyment; **broom**: a brush with a long handle used for cleaning floor; **mop**: a soft material attached to a handle, used for cleaning floors

More People Who Help Us

A **tailor** stitches our clothes and our school uniform. A **sewing machine** is used for stitching clothes.

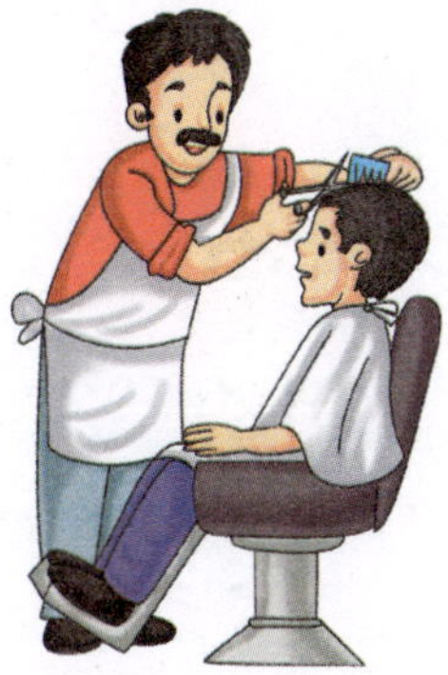

A **barber** cuts our hair. Barbers use **combs** and **scissors** to style and cut our hair.

A **grocer** sells things such as rice, sugar and tea.

A **greengrocer** sells fruits and vegetables.

A **postman** delivers letters to our home.

A **plumber** fixes and **repairs** the leaks in taps and pipes.

A **doctor** cures us when we are sick and gives us medicines.

A **cobbler** repairs broken shoes and slippers.

A **carpenter** makes and repairs wooden furniture using a saw, hammer and nails.

repair: to fix a thing that is broken or damaged so that we can use it again

Give it a shot

Match the people who help us with their tools or place of work.

1. 
2. 
3. 
4. 
5. 

a. 
b. 
c. 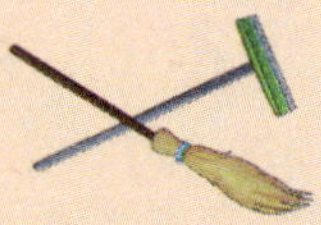
d. 
e. 

We should **respect** the people who work hard to make our lives comfortable. We should be good to people who help us. We must speak with them nicely and not be **rude** to them.

Think through

What would happen if we had to do all the work ourselves?

Wrap up

* There are many people around us who help us every day.
* These people help us at home, at school and in many other ways.
* We should respect and be kind to all the people who help us and make our lives easy.

Brush up

A Tick (✓) the correct answers.

1. A postman

   a. delivers milk b. delivers newspapers

   c. delivers letters d. cleans cars

rude: to say bad things to someone

2. A tailor
   a. cures us when we are sick
   b. stitches clothes
   c. makes furniture
   d. sweeps and cleans

3. A doctor
   a. cleans our cars
   b. fixes the taps
   c. cures us when we are sick
   d. fixes shoes

4. A teacher
   a. teaches us to read and write
   b. stitches clothes
   c. looks after the plants
   d. guards the school

5. A carpenter
   a. fixes leaking pipes and taps
   b. repairs torn shoes
   c. stitches our clothes
   d. makes furniture

B Fill in the blanks with the words given in the box.

cuts	cleans	furniture	fruits	vegetables	shoes

1. A sweeper .... our school.
2. A greengrocer sells .... and ....
3. A carpenter makes ....
4. A cobbler repairs ....
5. A barber .... hair.

C Answer these questions.

1. How does a doctor help us?
2. Name any two people who help us at home.
3. What does a plumber do?
4. What does the guard in the school do?
5. How should we behave with the people who help us?

Learn the ropes

Do you have a car cleaner or a maid at home? Are there any other helpers who work at your home? Find out their names and try to remember them. Write three ways in which you can show respect towards them.

Put your heads together

All the people living in a particular place make up a community. People who help us at homes, schools and in many other ways are also called community helpers. In groups of four, choose a community helper and collect pictures of the following:

a. type of work b. tools used c. uniforms

Paste these pictures in your notebook.

Cross connect

Find out the names of all the helpers who keep your school clean and take care of you in the school. Make Thank You cards for each one and give it to them.

13 Our House, Our Shelter

Get the ball rolling

What kind of houses are there near your house? What type of a house do you live in? Is it small or big?

We live with our family in a **house**. The house we live in becomes our **home**. Our house gives us **shelter** and protects us from the sun, rain, storms, cold, animals and thieves.

There are many types of houses. Some houses are big and some are small. Some houses are strong and some are not so strong. Houses can be of two types—**kutcha houses** or **pucca houses**.

Kutcha Houses

Kutcha houses are made of mud, straw and leaves. They are not very strong and are found mostly in villages.

Kutcha house

shelter: a place where we can stay safely

Huts are kutcha houses. The roofs of some huts are made of straw, twigs and leaves. These are called **thatched** roofs.

> **Clued in**
>
> Many years ago, people lived in caves because they did not know how to build houses.

Pucca Houses

Pucca houses are strong houses made of bricks, cement and steel. They can be big or small. Pucca houses can have **sloping** or **flat** roofs. Houses built on the mountains, or in places where it rains heavily usually have sloping roofs. This helps the snow and the rain to slide off. Pucca houses with flat roofs are found mostly in hot places where the land is flat.

House with a sloping roof

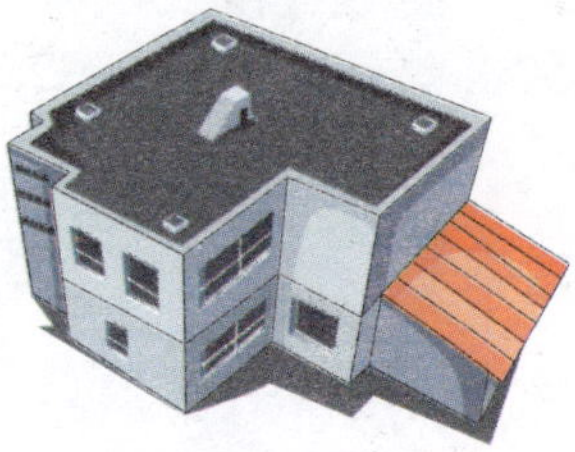

Double-storey house

Bungalow

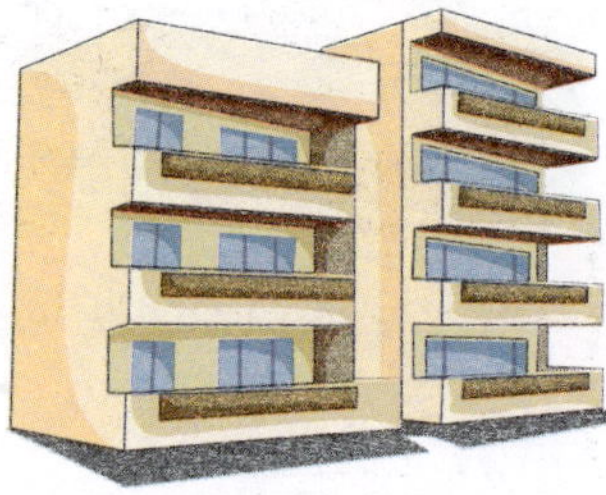

Apartment

Inside a House

There are many rooms inside a house. Each room is used for a different **purpose**.

We cook food in the **kitchen**.

purpose: the reason for which something is made or done

> **Give it a shot**
>
> Join the dots to complete the picture of the house and colour it.

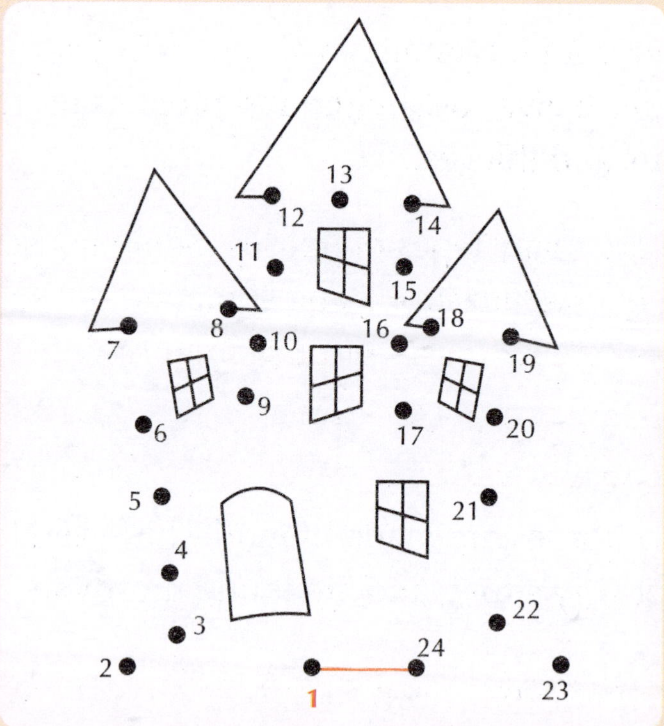

We eat meals with our family at the dining table in the **dining room**.

We sit with our guests in the **drawing room**.

We sleep and **relax** in the **bedroom**. We keep our clothes and toys in the cupboard in our bedroom.

We wash hands, brush teeth and take a bath in the **bathroom**.

We study, do homework and read books in the **study room**.

We watch television with our family and listen to music in the **living room**.

Houses are of different sizes. A house can have all of these rooms or some of these rooms.

Living room

Clean House

We should keep our house neat and clean. A house that is cleaned every day is a healthy house. A house should have enough windows. This allows sunlight and fresh air to come inside the house.

Think through

What are the three basic rooms that all houses have?

relax: to rest or do something enjoyable

Wrap up

- We live with our family in a house.
- A house protects us from sun, rain, storm, heat, cold, animals and thieves.
- Houses can be small or big.
- The two types of houses are kutcha house and pucca house.
- A house can have many rooms and each room has a different purpose.
- A house must have enough windows to let in sunlight and fresh air.
- It is important that we keep our house neat and clean.

Brush up

A **Put me in the correct room. Write the names of the rooms to which I belong.**

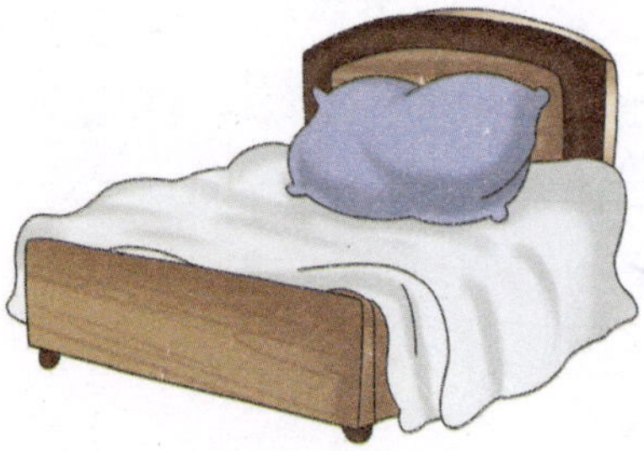

1. ....

2. ....

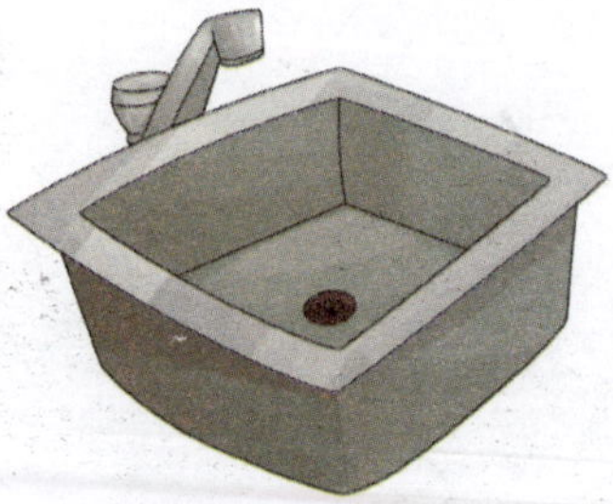

3. ....

4. ....

5. ....

B Fill in the blanks using the words given in the box.

sloping	strong	drawing room
study room	kutcha	living room

1. We sit with our guests in the ....
2. Houses made of mud and straw are called .... houses.
3. We study and read books in the ....
4. Houses made of bricks and cement are ....
5. Houses in places where it rains a lot have .... roofs.
6. We listen to music in the ....

C Answer these questions.

1. What are pucca houses made of?
2. What are kutcha houses made of?
3. Write the names of the rooms you have in your house. What are they used for?
4. Why do houses in the mountains have sloping roofs?
5. Why should houses have enough windows?

Learn the ropes

Make a list of the ways in which you try to keep your house or your room clean. Talk about these in class.

Put your heads together

In groups write a poem on your house and sing it together in class. You can start your poem like this:

Our house,
Is a very, very, very nice house...

Cross connect

Shape your house

Connect the shapes given here to the shapes in the picture and then colour the picture.

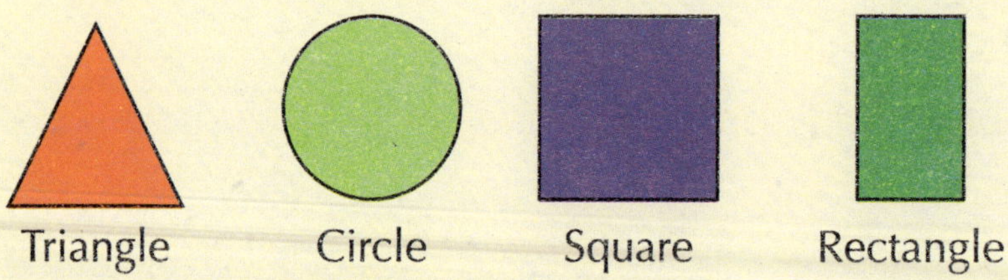

You can count the number of triangles and circles in this picture.

14 Weather and Seasons

Get the ball rolling

What do you see in these pictures?

A .... day

A .... day

The **condition** of the air at a place at a **particular** time is called **weather**. Weather changes every day. Some days are **sunny**, some are **cold**, some are **rainy** and some are **windy**. Weather can also change many times in a single day. It may be hot in the morning and suddenly it may get cold in the evening.

On a **hot day**, it is sunny and the Sun shines brightly in the sky. We wear light cotton clothes. We cover our head with caps, hats or **scarves**. We also carry an umbrella. We protect our eyes with sunglasses. We eat ice creams and drink cold juices on a hot day.

Think through

What do you like to eat in summer?

A hot day

condition: a state in which a thing is in; **particular**: about one thing; **scarf:** a piece of cloth round our neck or head

Clued in

Some places like Chennai do not have any winter. Leh hardly has any summer.

A cold day

A rainy day

On a **cold day**, it snows in some places. We wear warm woollen clothes, woollen caps, mufflers, socks and gloves to keep ourselves warm. We drink warm milk, hot soup, coffee or tea to keep our bodies warm on a cold day.

On a **rainy day**, it sometimes rains the whole day. We wear raincoats and **gumboots** to protect ourselves from the rain. We also carry umbrellas to keep our clothes from getting wet.

On a **windy day**, strong winds blow. They can carry things away with them. We should stay **indoors** on a windy day. This will keep us safe.

A windy day

gumboots: a pair of long rubber boots that are to keep feet from getting wet; **indoors**: inside a house or a building

Seasons

When the weather stays same for many days, it is called a **season**. There are five seasons in a year. They are spring, summer, monsoon, autumn and winter.

In the **spring**, flowers **bloom** and new leaves begin to grow on the trees.

In the **summer**, days are long and nights are short. It is the hottest time of the year.

In the **monsoon**, it rains a lot. It often rains the whole day.

In the **autumn**, the leaves of trees begin to change colour and fall off the trees.

In the **winter**, days are short and nights are long. Days and nights are very cold. We also see snow and **frost** in some places.

bloom: to produce flowers; **frost**: a thin white layer of ice that forms on the ground and other surfaces

Give it a shot

There are some pictures in the box given below. Write S for things used on a sunny day, R for things used on a rainy day and C for things used on a cold day.

1. 

Hot soup ☐

2. 

Ice cream ☐

3. 

Sunglasses ☐

4. 

Umbrella ☐

5. 

Slippers ☐

6. 

Gumboots ☐

7. 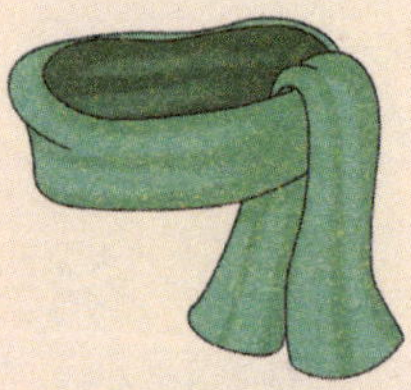

Muffler ☐

8. 

Raincoat ☐

9. 

Woollen cap ☐

10. 

Juice ☐

11. 

Coat ☐

12. 

Hat ☐

Wrap up

- The condition of the air at a place at a particular time is called weather.
- Weather may be sunny, hot, rainy, windy, cloudy or cold.
- When the weather stays same for many days, it is called a season.
- There are five seasons in a year. They are spring, summer, monsoon, autumn and winter.

Brush up

A Unscramble these words with the help of the clues.

1. SESONSA (When weather stays same for many days) ....
2. NETWIR (Days and nights are cold in this season) ....
3. GRINPS (Flowers bloom and new leaves grow on trees in this season) ....
4. MESRUM (Days and nights are hot during this season) ....
5. HEATREW (It may be sunny, windy, cloudy or cold) ....
6. TUMUNA (Trees shed their leaves during this season) ....

B Fill in the blanks with the correct answers.

1. When it is cold, in some places it .... (rains/snows)
2. The .... changes every day. (season/weather)
3. To protect ourselves from the rain, we need .... (sunglasses/raincoats)
4. We wear .... clothes to keep ourselves cool. (light/woollen)
5. Flowers bloom and new leaves begin to grow on the trees in .... (spring/winter)

C Answer these questions.

1. What are the different types of weather?

2. How can we keep ourselves warm on a cold day?
3. What is a season?

Learn the ropes

Observe the weather every day for a week. In your notebook, draw pictures of different types of weather you observe. You can draw rain, bright Sun or moving wind. At the end of the week, look at all the pictures and observe how the weather changes.

Put your heads together

Work in groups. Discuss with your group mates and choose a favourite weather. Draw pictures related to it and colour them. Share the pictures with other groups.

Cross connect

Ask your parents or your teacher to read the story, *The Ant and the Grasshopper* to you. Why do you think the little ant collects food in the summer and stores it for the winter?

15 Travel and Communicate

Get the ball rolling

How do you go to school every morning? Have you travelled by a train or an aeroplane? Discuss it in class.

We travel from one place to another for different reasons. Our parents travel to go to work and we travel to go to school. We also travel to different cities and countries.

Means of Transport

We can walk to places that are near our house. We travel in a **vehicle** to places that are far. These vehicles are called **means of transport**.

Different means of transport are used to travel to different places. Vehicles can move on land, on water and in the air.

vehicle: anything that carries people from one place to another

Vehicles on land

The vehicles that move on land are:

Car

Auto rickshaw

Motorcycle

Train

Metro

Bus

Cycle rickshaw

Most vehicles move on wheels. The bigger the vehicle, the more the number of wheels.

How many wheels does a cycle or a motorcycle have? ....

How many wheels does a car have? ....

How many wheels does a bus or a truck have? ....

Some vehicles that move on land are **drawn** by animals. Bullock cart and tonga are some examples.

Bullock cart

Vehicles on water

Some vehicles **sail** on water and help people cross rivers and seas. The vehicles that move on water are:

Ship

Boat

Steamer

drawn: to pull; **sail**: to move on water

Vehicles on Air

We can travel very fast and fly in the air like a bird. We can travel by an aeroplane to go from one place to another very quickly. Some vehicles that move in the air are:

Aeroplane

Helicopter

Rocket

The different means of transport have made our lives easy as we can reach any place easily.

> **Clued in**
>
> Vehicles that use petrol and diesel release smoke into the air. This makes the air dirty. We should try to walk or cycle and avoid using vehicles as much as we can.

Communication

When we travel, we stay in touch with our family so that they know where we are. We send them pictures when we are on a holiday. We also talk and write to our relatives about the fun things we do. When we talk, or write to someone it is called **communication**. The different ways we use to communicate are called **means of communication**. Let us learn more about them.

Staying in touch with family

> **Think through**
>
> Your mother wants to invite her friend to your birthday party. Which is the fastest means of communication that she can use to invite your friend?

Means of Communication

In the olden days, there were no phones and post offices. People would send messages through **pigeon posts** or **messengers**. Nowadays, we use fast means of communication. Some of them are telephones, mobile phones and computers. Television and radio are also important means of communication.

We can use a **telephone** to talk to another person in any part of the world.

We can talk to people across the world any time using a **mobile phone**. We can also send pictures, videos and text messages using a mobile phone.

We can send letters and messages through emails from our **computers** very quickly.

We get to know about events in our country and around the world on the **television** and **radio**.

We can send letters very quickly through **speed post** or **courier**.

We can read daily news and other entertaining things in a **newspaper**.

Can you name some more means of communication?

We should be polite when communicating. We should listen first and then talk.

pigeon posts: the use of pigeons to carry messages; **messengers**: people who gives messages to others

Give it a shot

Colour the box below each vehicle and the means of communication using the following key:

- Blue: Fastest way to send a message
- Orange: Two-wheeled vehicle
- Green: Four-wheeled vehicle
- Pink: We can watch news on this
- Purple: We use this to send emails
- Yellow: Three-wheeled vehicle

Wrap up

* We need transport to travel from one place to another.
* We use different means of transport to travel to different places.
* Vehicles can move on land, on water and in air.
* Some vehicles like bullock cart and tonga are drawn by animals.
* When we talk or write to someone, it is called communication.
* We use different means to communicate different things.
* Nowadays, the means of communication are very fast.

Brush up

A Write the names of the means of transport you would use to go to these places.

1. From Delhi to London to meet your uncle ....
2. To school ....
3. To a store in the market near your house ....
4. To meet your grandmother who lives in another city
   ....
5. To the park in your neighbourhood ....

B Fill in the blanks using the words given in the box.

television	mobile phone	communication	pigeon posts	speed post

1. In the olden days people sent messages to others by ....
   ....
2. When we talk or write to someone, it is called ....
3. Nowadays, we can quickly send a message using a ....
   ....
4. We use .... to send letters quickly.
5. We get to know a lot of things from the ....

C Answer these questions.

1. What are means of transport?
2. What is communication?
3. Write the names of one vehicle each that moves on land, water and air.
4. How did people in the old days send messages to each other?
5. Name any two vehicles that are pulled by animals.
6. Write the names of one means of communication each that we can use to read only, hear only and talk only.

Learn the ropes

Which vehicle do you have at home? Every vehicle has a number that is given on a number plate. Do you know the number of your vehicle? Find out from your home. If you do not own a vehicle, find out your school bus number with the help of your teacher.

Put your heads together

Work in groups. Ask your teacher to help you draw and cut shapes using a coloured paper. Each group should have one or more of the following shapes – square, circle, triangle and rectangle. Put these shapes together to make a means of transport. Stick the pieces together on a paper and play the game of Show and Tell in class. Take turns and show the means of transport to the other groups and they can guess their names.

Cross connect

Different vehicles make different sounds. For example, a train whistles and cars, buses and trucks blow horn. Ambulances and police cars have a siren. Now imagine what these sounds would look like if you were to draw them. Using crayons and paper draw the sounds made by the different means of transport.

16 The Earth and the Sky

Get the ball rolling

Why does the sky look different during the day and at the night? Discuss in class.

The Earth

We live on the **Earth**. It is covered with land and water. It has more water than land. The Earth has air, water, heat and light, which help plants and animals live.

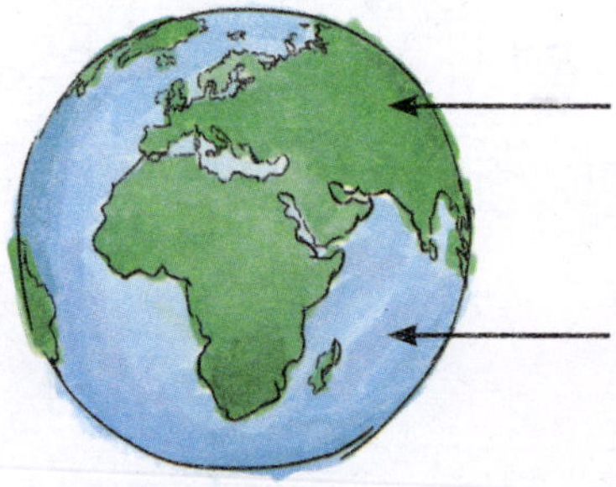

The Earth

Have you seen a globe? A sphere-shaped model of the Earth is called the **globe**. If you turn the globe around its starts spinning. The Earth **spins** the same way, just like a top.

A globe

Clued in

The Earth moves continuously around the Sun.

spin: to turn quickly around a central point

The land

Land has many shapes and forms. It has forests and flat lands. In some places it is raised.

An area of land where many trees grow is called a **forest**. Many animals live in a forest.

Flat lands are called **plains**.

Raised but not very high parts of land are called **hills**.

A forest

A plain

Hills

Raised and very high parts of land are called **mountains**.

There are **valleys** between the hills and the mountains.

Land which is dry and covered with sand is called a **desert**.

Mountains

Valleys

Desert

Water on the Earth

Water is present on the Earth in **rivers**, **lakes**, **ponds**, **seas** and **oceans**. It is also found in the form of **snow** on mountains. Water is also found under the ground. Many plants and animals live in water.

River

Lake

Pond

Ocean

Sea

The Sky

The space above the Earth is the sky. We can see the Sun, the Moon, the stars and the clouds in the sky.

During the day, the Sun shines brightly in the sky. The sky appears blue. We see white **fluffy** clouds in the sky. Sometimes we see a **rainbow** in the sky after it rains. It has seven colours.

> **Think through**
>
> Why is the Sun important to us?

At night, the sky is dark. Stars **twinkle** and the Moon shines in the night sky. The shape of the Moon changes every night. We cannot see the Sun at night.

The day sky

The night sky

fluffy: light and soft, looking like cotton; **twinkle**: shining

Give it a shot

There are seven colours in a rainbow. Now, colour this rainbow using crayons.

1	Red
2	Orange
3	Yellow
4	Green
5	Blue
6	Indigo
7	Violet

Days and Weeks

One **day** is equal to 24 hours. It has morning, afternoon, evening and night. A period of seven days, from Monday to Sunday, forms one **week**. The days of the week are Monday, Tuesday, Wednesday, Thursday, Friday, Saturday and Sunday. One year has 365 days and 52 weeks.

Wrap up

* We live on the Earth. It is covered with land and water.
* Land has forest, plains, mountains, hills, valleys and deserts.
* Water has rivers, lakes, ponds, seas and oceans.
* The space above the Earth is the sky.
* There are Sun, Moon, stars and clouds in the sky.
* The sky looks different during the day and at night.
* A night and a day is equal to twenty-four hours.
* A week is a period of seven days, from Monday to Sunday.
* One year has 365 days and 52 weeks.

Brush up

A **Tick (✓) the correct sentences and cross (×) the wrong ones.**

1. Many plants and animals live in water. ☐
2. The moon has light of its own. ☐
3. Flat lands are called plains. ☐
4. A rainbow has seven colours and looks beautiful. ☐

B **Fill in the blanks with the correct answers.**

1. During the day the colour of the sky is .... (green/blue)
2. A piece of land with many trees is called .... (desert/forest)
3. Land which is covered with sand is called .... (desert/forest)
4. The Earth is covered with land and .... (water/light)

C **Answer these questions.**

1. What is the Earth made up of?
2. How is the sky different in the day from the sky at night?
3. What are days and weeks?
4. Where does water exist on the Earth?

Learn the ropes

Discuss with your teacher the ways to keep the Earth clean. Write three points and draw and paste pictures to explain each point.

Put your heads together

Work in groups. Note down three interesting activities you did in class in one week. On a drawing sheet, draw pictures related to these activities. Paint to make the chart colourful.

Cross connect

Make a colourful drawing of a place you have visited recently. It can be a picnic spot, valley, a forest, a sea or a beach.

17 Our Festivals

Get the ball rolling

What are these pictures showing us? Which of these festivals do you celebrate? Is there any other festival that you celebrate? Talk about it in class.

Festivals are special days of the year celebrated by everyone. People **celebrate** and have fun during festivals. During festivals people wear new clothes, eat special food, meet their family and friends and exchange gifts. We celebrate many festivals in India.

Holi

Holi is the festival of colours. People put colours on each other on Holi. They also spray coloured water using a spraygun or *pichkari*. Holi is celebrated at the beginning of the spring season. A special sweet called *gujiya* is eaten on this day.

Holi

celebrate: to enjoy with family and friends

Diwali

Diwali is the festival of lights. On this day, Lord Ram returned to Ayodhya after living in a forest for 14 years. People **decorate** their homes on Diwali with flowers, lights, candles and *diyas*. They pray to Goddess Lakshmi and Lord Ganesha.

Diwali

Eid ul-Fitr

Eid ul-Fitr

Eid ul-Fitr is celebrated at the end of the holy month of Ramzan. People go to the mosque and pray, wear new clothes and wish each other 'Eid Mubarak'. Many people make a special sweet dish called *seviyan* on this day.

Clued in

In India, we celebrate many harvest festivals. These are celebrated all over the country with different names.

Gurpurab

The birthday of the Sikh Gurus is celebrated as **Gurpurab**. People decorate their houses with lights and go to gurdwaras to pray. They are given *karha prasad* or *halwa*. They also eat *langar*, which is a free meal served in gurdwaras.

Gurpurab

Christmas

Christmas

The birthday of Jesus Christ is celebrated as **Christmas** on 25 December every year. People decorate their houses and the Christmas tree. They go to the church and pray and **exchange** gifts. Children wait for Santa Claus to bring them gifts.

decorate: to make something look beautiful; **exchange**: to give something and get something else in return

Give it a shot

Make your own festival album. Find pictures of different festivals that you have celebrated with your family, friends and relatives and paste them in a scrapbook. Write the name of the festival that was celebrated under the picture. Also, write what you did on that day.

National Festivals

There are some special days in the year that are important to our country. These are our **national festivals** and are celebrated by everyone in the country.

Think through

How should we greet and wish others on different festivals?

Independence Day

Independence Day is celebrated every year on 15 August. We **hoist** the national flag and sing the national anthem on this day.

Republic Day

Republic Day is celebrated on 26 January every year. India became a **republic** on this day.

2 October is celebrated as **Gandhi Jayanti** every year. This is the birthday of Mahatma Gandhi, the father of our nation.

Mahatma Gandhi, father of our nation

Festivals are **special** and we should **respect** all festivals. We should greet and wish our family, friends, teachers and others in the school on these festivals.

hoist: to pull something up high; **republic:** a country where power is held by the people or their chosen people

Wrap up

- Festivals are special days that everyone celebrates.
- Some festivals that we all enjoy are Holi, Diwali, Eid ul-Fitr, Gurpurab and Christmas.
- There are also some important days for our country which all the people of the country celebrate. These are our national festivals.

Brush up

A **Match the festival with its special food. Then unscramble the given letters to find the names of the festivals.**

1. 	a.		MHACRSITS	....
2. 	b.		IDE-LU-TRIF	....
3. 	c.		HILO	....
4. 	d.		ILDWAI	....

B Draw a for the true sentences and a for the false ones.

1. Santa Claus brings gifts for children on Christmas.
2. India became a republic on 15 August.
3. *Karha prasad* is a free meal served in gurdwaras.
4. People wish each other 'Eid Mubarak' on Eid ul-Fitr.
5. Gandhi Jayanti is celebrated on 2 October.

C Answer these questions.

1. What is a festival?
2. How do people celebrate festivals?
3. Name the national festivals celebrated in our country.
4. What should we do on every festival?

Learn the ropes

Holi is a festival of colour and friendship. However, there are some people who throw water-filled balloons and eggs on people on the streets even before Holi. What will you do to make sure that you celebrate all festivals safely?

Put your heads together

The colours used for Holi can be harmful to us. We can make natural Holi colours that do not have chemicals and do not harm us. These are also good for the environment as they are made from natural things. Work in groups. Bring flour, turmeric powder and henna from home. Mix the flour and henna and flour and turmeric powder separately to make natural green and yellow Holi colours.

Cross connect

Get your classroom ready to celebrate Diwali. You can decorate your classroom with brightly-coloured diyas. Bring terracotta diyas from home. Using colours, paint them with your favourite colours. Keep them aside for some time till they dry. Now arrange all the diyas in the classroom and get ready to celebrate Diwali!

18 Safety Rules

Get the ball rolling

Look at the pictures. Put a tick (✓) if it is a safe thing or a cross (×) if it is not.

Safety means being safe from danger or getting hurt. We should keep ourselves safe by being careful. We must learn to follow safety rules.

Safety at Home

Stay away from fire and do not touch hot objects.

Never open doors to strangers.

Keep away from electrical items. Do not touch electrical **sockets** or wires.

Do not use sharp objects like scissors, knife and blade.

Do not **lean** over balcony **railings**.

Safety on Roads

Always step out of your home with an adult.

Always walk on the **pavement** or on the side of the road. Do not play on the road or on the pavement.

Always cross the road at the **zebra crossing**.

Traffic Lights

We should always follow the **traffic lights** while on the road. Red light indicates 'stop'. Yellow light indicates 'wait'. Green light indicates 'go'.

Traffic lights

Crossing the road

We should always hold the hand of an adult while crossing the road. We should cross only when the **pedestrian** light turns green.

Before crossing, look to your right, then to your left and once again to your right. If the road is clear, cross the road.

> **Clued in**
>
> Zebra crossings have black and white stripes on the road, just like the stripes of a zebra.

sockets: a device in a wall that you put a plug into; **lean**: to bend; **railing**: a fence made of metal bars; **pavement**: footpath; **pedestrian**: a person walking and not travelling in a vehicle

Safety in School

We should enter the class in a queue

We should always wait for our turn to play on the swings or slides in the playground. We should never stand too close to the swings.

We should always walk in a **queue**.

We should never push each other.

We should never jump on chairs or tables.

Give it a shot

Discuss and make five safety rules you would follow in the classroom. Write them down on a sheet of paper and put it on the class display board. You can also draw pictures of Do's and Don'ts on the chart.

Safety in Bus or Car

We should wear seat belt in a car

To remain safe in a bus or a car wait in a line for the bus to arrive. Never push anyone while boarding the bus.

Never stick your hands or head out of a moving bus or a car.

Always wait for a bus or a car to stop before getting off.

Always wear a **seat belt** in the car.

Safety While Swimming

We should wear swim rings

Always go with an adult for a swim.

If you are learning to swim, use **swim rings**.
Do not try to jump or go towards the area where water is deep.

queue: a line of people; **seat belt**: a belt that is attached to the seat in a car that you fasten around yourself; **swim rings**: air-filled rings which are worn around the waist to keep a person above water

First Aid

First aid is the help given to an injured person before the arrival of a doctor. If a person gets hurt, inform an adult **immediately**. If the person is not hurt badly, a basic first aid helps. A first aid box must be kept in class, home as well as in the car.

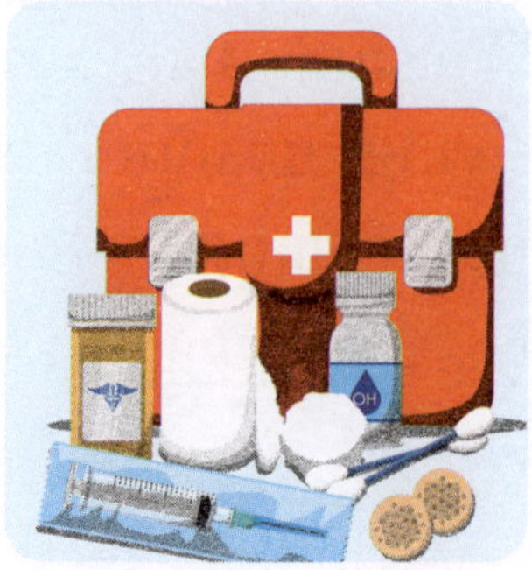

First aid kit

Be Safe

- Do not take anything from strangers.
- Do not go out with strangers, if someone forces you to do so, scream at the top your voice.
- Do not touch anything lying around in the park, playground or road.

Think through

Why should we not touch anything lying around in the park, playground or road?

Wrap up

* Safety means being safe from danger or getting hurt.
* We must learn to follow safety rules at all times.
* We should be careful and be safe at home, on roads, in school, on a bus, in a car and while swimming.
* We should always cross the roads at zebra crossings.
* First aid is the help given to an injured person before the arrival of a doctor.

Brush up

A Fill in the blanks with the correct answers.

1. Always step out of your home with an .... (adult/umbrella)
2. Do not take anything from .... (parents/strangers)
3. We should .... push each other. (never/sometimes)

immediately: at once

4. Never stick out your .... out of a moving vehicle. (tongue/hand)

B **Tick (✓) the correct sentences and cross (×) the wrong ones.**

1. We should always wait for our turn to board a bus. ☐
2. We should never stay away from fire and always touch hot objects. ☐
3. We must not go out with strangers. ☐
4. If someone gets hurt, we should inform the teacher or an adult after an hour. ☐

C **Answer these questions.**

1. What do you understand by safety?
2. What is first aid?
3. What are the safety rules that should be followed in school?

Learn the ropes

You must have heard about the new virus, that is making everyone sick. Make posters on ways to be safe from covid 19.

Put your heads together

In groups, make a first aid box for your classroom. You can bring things such as bandages, antiseptics and medicines to put in it from home.

Cross connect

Think of a story about a child who forgot to follow traffic light and traffic rules while playing. Enact a play on traffic rules in your classroom.

Our National Symbols

The National Flag

Every country has national symbols. A flag is a symbol of a country. The Indian national flag is also called the **tricolour** as it has three colours. These are saffron, white and green. The **Ashoka Chakra** is in the middle of the flag. It has 24 spokes. The colours in our national flag have special meaning. Saffron stands for **courage** and **sacrifice**. White stands for **peace** and **purity**. Green means **growth** and **prosperity**. We must respect our national flag.

Tricolour

Some more national symbols of our country are:

National animal

Royal Bengal Tiger

National flower

Lotus

National bird

Peacock

National tree

Banyan

National river

Ganga

National fruit

Mango

courage: to do something without fear; **sacrifice**: to give up something that is important to you; **prosperity**: to be successful

The National Anthem

Our national anthem is **Jana Gana Mana**. It was written by Rabindranath Tagore. We must stand whenever our national anthem is played as a mark of respect to our country. The national anthem is sung at the end of important functions in school like the assemblies and annual celebrations. It is also sung on important national days.

Rabindranath Tagore

Jana-gana-mana-adhinayaka jaya he
Bharata-bhagya-vidhata
Panjaba-Sindhu-Gujarata-Maratha
Dravida-Utkala-Banga
Vindhya-Himachala-Yamuna-Ganga
uchchala-jaladhi-taranga
Tava Subha name jage, tave subha asisa mage,
gahe tava jaya-gatha.
Jana-gana-mangala-dayaka jaya he
Bharata-bhagya-vidhata.
Jaya he, Jaya he, Jaya he,
jaya jaya jaya jaya he.

The National Emblem

The national emblem of India is an **adaptation** of the **Lion Capital of Ashoka**. It is a **sculpture** that has four Asiatic lions standing back to back. Below the lions, is the Ashoka Chakra.

The Lion Capital of Ashoka

adaptation: to change a particular piece of work for a new situation; **sculpture:** a figure or an object made by carving or shaping stone

Hand Washing Steps

Follow these steps while washing your hands.

Palm to palm

Wrists

Fingers interlaced

Fingernails

Back of hands

Back of fingers

Base of thumbs

Wash your hands often

We should always wash our hands. Colour this page.

Suggested Assessment 1

A Choose the correct word and name the given pictures.

Tree Raincoat Bathroom Small family Summer

1. ....

2. ....

3. ....

4. ....

5. ....

B Match the following.

1.  a. Grandmother

2.  b. Washing hair

3.  c. Shrub

4.  d. Fruits

5. 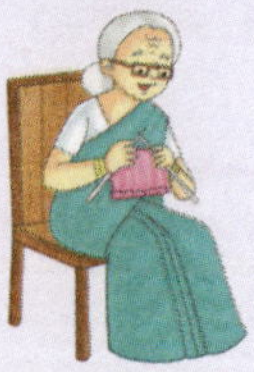 e. Tongue helps to taste

C Tick (✓) the odd one out in each set.

1.

a. ☐ b. ☐ c. ☐ d. ☐

2.

a. ☐ b. ☐ c. ☐ d. ☐

3.

a. ☐ b. ☐ c. ☐ d. ☐

4.

a. ☐ b. ☐ c. ☐ d. ☐

D Draw 🙂 for correct sentence and ☹ for the wrong ones.

1. Markets are not needed in neighbourhoods. ◯
2. A greengrocer sells things like rice, sugar and tea. ◯
3. Kutcha houses have a thatched roof. ◯
4. Weather never changes. ◯
5. Vehicles can only move on land. ◯

Suggested Assessment 2

A Fill in the blanks.

1. Our teachers teach us .... and to be well ....
2. We go to the .... when we are badly hurt.
3. A .... and a .... are people who help us in school.
4. The different rooms inside a house are used for a different ....
5. We wear .... clothes during the summer.

B Tick (✓) the correct answers.

1. People travel from one place to another to
   a. go for a walk b. go for a holiday c. play in the park
2. We can live on the Earth because
   a. it spins like a top b. it is covered with water
   c. it has land, water, heat and light.
3. On this festival, people decorate their homes with lights, candles and diyas
   a. Christmas b. Eid ul-Fitr c. Diwali
4. To be safe at home we must
   a. not open doors to strangers b. lean over balconies c. use the gas stove
5. The national anthem of India was written by
   a. Bankim Chandra Chatterjee b. Sarojini Naidu c. Rabindranath Tagore

C Look at the pictures and complete the names of the seasons.

1. ....U M........ ....

2. W........N........E........

3. S........R........N........

4. A U........ ....N

5. M O........S........ ....N